AFRAID

Copyright © 1991 Steck-Vaughn Company

Copyright © 1991 Raintree Publishers Limited Partnership

Copyright © Cherrytree Press Ltd 1990

First published 1990
by Cherrytree Press Ltd
Windsor Bridge Road
Bath, Avon BA2 3AX England

First published in the United States 1991
by Raintree Publishers, A Division of Steck-Vaughn Company

Library of Congress Number: 90-46540

Library of Congress Cataloging-in-Publication Data

Amos, Janine.
  Feelings/by Janine Amos; illustrated by Gwen Green.
  Cover title.
  Contents: [1] Afraid—[2] Angry—[3] Hurt—[4] Jealous—[5] Lonely—[6] Sad.
  1. Emotions—Case studies—Juvenile literature. [1. Emotions.] I. Green, Gwen, ill. II.
Title.
BF561.A515   1991
152.4—dc20
                                            90-46540
                                                 CIP
                                                 AC

ISBN 0-8172-3775-5   hardcover library binding
ISBN 0-8114-6908-5   softcover binding

Other hardcover ISBNs: Angry   0-8172-3776-3   Lonely 0-8172-3779-8
                               Hurt   0-8172-3777-1   Sad   0-8172-3780-1
                               Jealous   0-8172-3778-X

4 5 6 7 8 9   95

AFRAID

By Janine Amos
Illustrated by Gwen Green

RSVP
RAINTREE
STECK-VAUGHN
PUBLISHERS
The Steck-Vaughn Company

Austin, Texas

TONY'S STORY

One night Tony couldn't get to sleep. His head was full of ideas. Mostly he was thinking about a ghost he'd seen in one of his comic books. The more he thought about the picture of the ghost, the harder it was to go to sleep.

Tony tossed and turned. He opened his eyes and looked around the dark room. What was that shape in the corner? Tony started to feel afraid.

It seemed to Tony that something or someone was in his bedroom, but it was too dark to see. Was that breathing he heard?

He slid way down under the covers.

"Mom! I don't feel good!" he shouted.

Tony's mother switched on the bedroom light. Tony saw his own, safe bedroom all around him, and he felt much better.

"What's the matter, Tony?" asked his mother. But Tony didn't want to tell her.

"Well, you were probably dreaming," she said, as she went out the door. "Go back to sleep now."

"Don't shut the door!" called Tony. "Leave it open a little, please, just in case I feel sick again." He could see the light outside his door, and he wasn't afraid.

Why didn't Tony tell his mother how he was feeling?
How do you think his mother feels right now?

The next day Tony had a great time. He played with his friends. But when bedtime came, he said that he didn't feel tired.

"Go upstairs and read, then," said his mother. "You'll fall asleep soon."

"I just want to see the rest of this show," said Tony.

At the end of the TV program, he wanted a drink. Then he wanted to get some things ready to take to school.

"Enough!" said his mother. "Go to bed. Now!"

Tony walked slowly upstairs. When he got into bed, he left the door open, with the hall light on. Soon his mother went to bed, too. She turned off all the lights.

Tony lay in the dark. Things seemed to be moving around the room. Was it the ghost? Tony couldn't keep still. He jumped out of bed and turned on the light.

If you were Tony, what would you do now?

Tony looked around his room. All his things were right where he had left them. He couldn't see anything unusual or bad anywhere in the room. He went back to bed. After a while, he fell asleep with the light on.

When Tony woke up in the morning, his brother Pete was sitting on the bed. He gave Tony a glass of juice.

"How come you left your light on all night?" asked Pete.

Tony blushed. "I must have forgotten," he said.

"Listen, Tony," said Pete. "It's okay. Lots of people are scared of the dark sometimes. I was for a while."

"You were?" asked Tony. "I know it's dumb, but I really did think there was something in my room. I'm afraid of the dark." He started to cry.

"You won't be afraid tonight, I promise," said Pete. "Now that you've told me, we can do something about it."

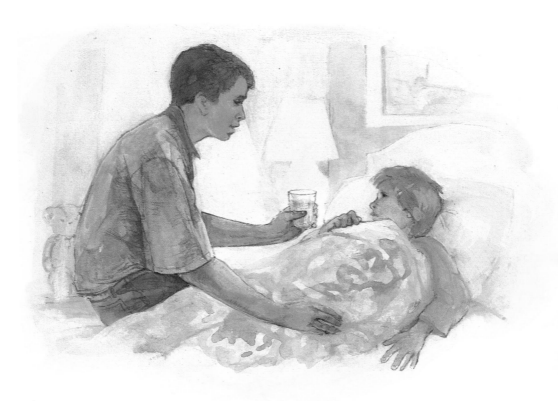

That night when Tony went to bed, Pete went up with him.

"Tell me about the thing in your room," Pete said. "Was it green and hairy?"

"No," said Tony. "It was gray." He showed Pete the comic book.

"Oh, him!" said Pete. "I saw him in the bathroom a minute ago. He was brushing his teeth!"

Tony laughed. His brother always made him laugh. But it made Tony feel better. He climbed into bed.

"I'll leave your door open," said Pete, "and the hall light on. Then the ghost can see where it's going, so it won't stub its toe!"

Tony giggled, and soon he fell sound asleep.

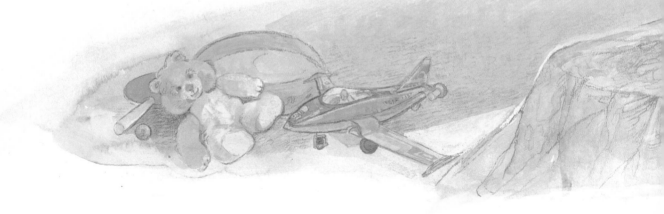

How did Pete help Tony? Who would you talk to if you felt afraid?

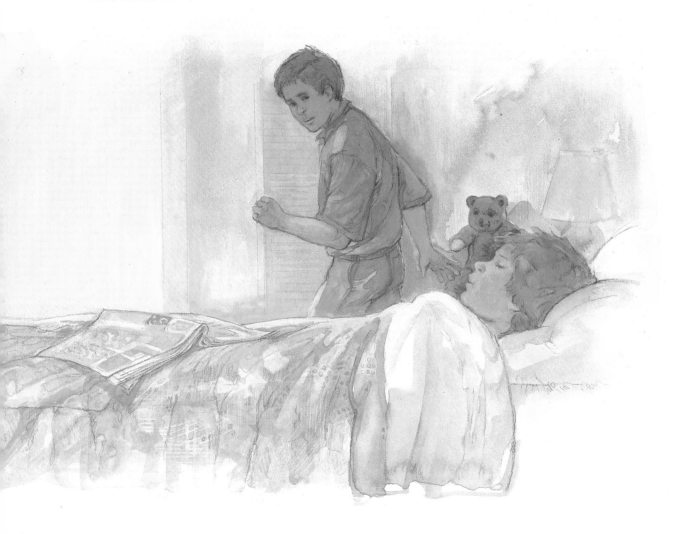

Feeling like Tony

Have you ever felt afraid, the way Tony did? Nearly everyone feels frightened sometimes. It feels even worse when you know that there's really nothing to be scared of, but you still can't stop yourself from being afraid.

It helps to talk

Fears grow when you keep them to yourself. The best thing to do is talk about feeling afraid. Tell someone you trust. Don't be scared that other people will laugh at you. Only mean or silly people do that.

Feeling scared is natural

Sometimes there are good reasons to be scared. Sometimes dogs *do* bite. Sometimes people *do* slip on ice. Fear is natural. It is sensible to be careful when you see a stray dog or walk on an icy sidewalk. But there is no point in being scared for no reason.

Think about it

Read the stories in this book. Think about the people in the stories. Do you sometimes feel the way they do? Remember what you did the last time you were afraid. Think what is the best thing to do. Next time you feel scared, ask yourself some questions: Why am I afraid? Can what I'm scared of really happen? Who can I tell? Then talk to someone, just as Tony did.

ROSA'S STORY

"Have a good day at school, Rosa!" her mother said.

Rosa stood at the edge of the school yard and waved to her mother. Soon the car was out of sight. Just then a loud voice called.

"There she is!"

Rosa started to run, but it was too late. Four big girls stood around her. Rosa felt very small. She was afraid.

"Give us your money," said one of the bigger girls. Rosa felt the coins in her pocket. She closed her hand around them tightly.

"No," she said. The big girls came closer.

"Come on. Hand it over. Now!" they said.

One of the girls grabbed Rosa's arm and squeezed hard. Rosa could feel tears filling her eyes. She wanted to yell. Instead, she held out her hand, and another girl grabbed the money. Then the biggest girl shoved Rosa.

"Don't tell anyone, or you'll be sorry!" the girl shouted. Then the four girls ran away.

How do you think Rosa feels right now?

Rosa hurried into her classroom. Mrs. Young, her teacher, smiled at her.

"You're here early, Rosa," said Mrs. Young.

Quickly, Rosa took out her reading book. She pretended she was finishing a story. Really, she was thinking about the bullies. They had taken her lunch money. They had done it last week, too. Rosa thought about them all morning.

At lunchtime, Rosa felt sad.

"What's wrong?" asked her friend Jo. "You can tell me." So Rosa told Jo what had happened.

"We have to tell Mrs. Young," said Jo. Rosa knew that Jo was right, but she was still afraid.

"First, though, we'll share my lunch," Jo said.

Rosa and Jo found Mrs. Young in the classroom. Together they told her how the big girls had bullied Rosa.

"Can you tell me what they look like?" Mrs. Young asked. Rosa remembered the biggest girl who had shoved her and the one with the spiky hair.

"I know which girls you mean," said Mrs. Young. "You did the right thing in telling me. Now, don't worry. I'll take care of those girls."

Do you think Rosa and Jo were right to tell Mrs. Young? What do you think Mrs. Young will say to the bullies?

After school, Jo waited with Rosa until Rosa's mother arrived. The girls who had bullied Rosa hurried past them.

"There they go," whispered Rosa. But now the big girls didn't seem frightening. They had their heads down, and they didn't even look at Rosa.

"They're ashamed of themselves," said Jo.

Why isn't Rosa frightened now? How do you think the bullies feel?

Feeling like Rosa

The bigger girls knew Rosa was afraid of them. They knew that they could make her give them her money. They tried to make her so scared that she would never tell on them. Have you ever been afraid of someone, like Rosa was? Do you know any bullies who get their own way by frightening others? Most bullies are older and stronger than the people they pick on. Some adults are bullies, too.

Speak out!

Keeping quiet helps bullies. It gives them power. But you can take that power away from them just by talking. The best thing to do if you feel afraid like Rosa is to talk to someone who can help, like a parent or a teacher. Don't help bullies by keeping them a secret.

SIMON'S STORY

Simon was having fun. He was in the park with his friends. They were playing soccer, and Simon's team was winning. Some of the parents were cheering from the sidelines.

"Pass the ball, Simon!" someone shouted.

Simon was just about to kick the ball. But then a big white dog raced onto the field. Simon left the ball and ran. The dog chased after him.

"Mom!" shouted Simon.

Simon threw himself at his mother.

"It's all right," she said. "He wanted to play, that's all. Look, he's gone now."

Simon watched the big dog trotting away.

When they got home after the game, Simon's dad had some news.

"Here's a letter from Uncle Jerry. He's coming to stay with us in a couple of weeks," he said.

"Great!" said Simon. Jerry was his favorite uncle.

"This time," said his dad, "Uncle Jerry is bringing his dog."

"But I don't like dogs!" shouted Simon. "Tell Uncle Jerry we can't have a dog here!"

"I think maybe you need to know more about dogs," said Simon's dad. "Then they won't seem so frightening."

How do you think Simon felt when he heard there would be a dog staying at his house?

The next day Simon and his dad went to the library. They went to a shelf marked "Pets." Simon's dad opened a big book and pointed to a yellow dog.

"Look, Simon," he said. "That's a Labrador retriever. It's the same kind of dog as Uncle Jerry's. Why don't we check this book out?"

At home, Simon looked at the book with his dad.

"How big is a Labrador?" asked Simon.

"Well, when it's standing up, its head would probably reach above your waist," his dad replied. Simon groaned.

"I wish Uncle Jerry had a kitten or a rabbit."

Simon and his dad looked at the book every evening. By Saturday, Simon had learned a lot about Labradors.

"We'd better do some extra shopping for Uncle Jerry's visit," said Simon's mom. "I'll need your help, Simon, now that you're the expert on what dogs eat."

At the supermarket, Simon lifted the cans of dog food off the shelves and put them in the cart.

"What is Uncle Jerry's dog's name?" he asked.

"I think she's called Sheba," said his mom.

"Sheba," Simon repeated in a whisper.

The day that Uncle Jerry was due to arrive, Simon woke up early. He couldn't wait! At last, a car pulled into the driveway, and Simon raced to the door.

"Remember," warned his dad, "don't jump around too much and get Sheba excited."

Simon ran up to the car. He saw Sheba standing in the back. Her tail was wagging. She didn't look too fierce.

While Uncle Jerry told everyone about his trip, Sheba looked around the house. She sniffed at Simon's sports bag.

"She can smell your soccer shoes!" said Simon's mom.

Simon watched Uncle Jerry stroking Sheba.

"You can pet her if you want to," said Uncle Jerry.

"Not yet," said Simon.

How do you think Simon feels now?

Simon went along when Uncle Jerry took Sheba for a walk. They threw sticks, and Sheba brought them back in her mouth. Simon enjoyed the game. Soon he was running ahead to look for more sticks. Then he heard Sheba panting close behind. Simon wasn't sure what to do. He ran faster, and so did Sheba. Then Simon heard Uncle Jerry calling.

"Slow down, Simon! She's only playing."

Simon stopped running, and Sheba stopped too.

Why do you think Sheba was chasing after Simon? What should Simon do now?

"Did she scare you?" asked Uncle Jerry.

"Not really," said Simon, stroking Sheba's ears. "She just got excited."

Simon looked down at Sheba's silky head.

"I'm glad you brought Sheba with you," he said. "I know more about dogs now."

"And when you're playing and a strange dog runs up, what will you do?" asked Uncle Jerry.

"I'll stand still until it goes away!" said Simon.

How did Sheba's visit help Simon?

Feeling like Simon

Have you ever felt afraid of an animal, like Simon did? Some people are afraid of spiders or wasps or cats. Whenever they see one, they panic. Simon needed to learn more about dogs. By getting to know more about the things he feared, Simon was able to relax. Of course, it makes sense to be careful when a strange dog runs up to you. But it doesn't help to get upset. It's the same with any other fear. You need to try not to panic. Think what you can do about your problem.

Feeling afraid

Think about the stories in this book. Tony, Rosa, and Simon were each afraid of different things. And they each found someone to help them. If you say, "I'm afraid," someone will help you, too.

Asking for help

It's often hard to tell someone else that you're afraid. But talking to someone you trust makes you feel stronger. You may have to ask for help, like Rosa did. We all need help sometimes.

Keep trying

Rosa was lucky. Her teacher had time to listen. But if the first person you talk to can't help, try someone else. Tell a neighbor or friend or parent about your fear. There is always someone who can help.

If you are feeling frightened or unhappy, don't keep it to yourself. Talk to an adult you can trust:

- one of your parents or other relatives
- a friend's parent or other relative
- a teacher
- the principal
- someone else at school
- a neighbor
- someone at a church, temple, or synagogue

You can also find someone to talk to about a problem by calling places called "hotlines." One hotline is **Child Help,** which you can call from anywhere in the United States. Just call

1-800-422-4453

from any telephone. You don't need money to call.

Or look in the phone book to find another phone number of people who can help. Try

- Children and Family Service
- Family Service

Remember you can always call the Operator in any emergency. Just dial 0 or press the button that says 0 on the telephone.